Practical Advice
about
Things you need to know
before you Startup

Your Startup Mentor

Mukesh Gupta

Your Startup Mentor

Your Startup Mentor

Things You need to Know
before you Startup

- Mukesh Gupta

Copyright 2015 Mukesh Gupta

All rights reserved

**Dedicated
To All My Friends
Who want to
Startup and Make the world a
Better Place**

Contents:

Preface to this edition

The Search

Introduction

The Meeting

The Why

The When

The How

Product or Service

Funding

Building a team

Keys to Staying in Business

Compensation

Competition

Winding Up

Thanks

The Search

I have searched for a teacher far and wide

Read countless books & blogs

Listened to countless men & their podcasts

Talk about starting and running a business!

But I am yet to meet a man

Who's done it all

Ran some successfully

Sold some successfully,

Lost money in some

Is humble, Is wise

And willing to share his wisdom!

Introduction

One day, a friend of mine

told me about an old man

Who had started a number of businesses

Some highly successful & some barely so

Some utterly failing & some marginally so

Some he sold for a killing

& some just to stay afloat

He was open and willing to share his wisdom

With anyone who was willing to probe

So, with not much expectation

I ask for an audience!

Pat comes the reply -

"Anytime that suits you"

The meeting:

So, with a pen and a paper

And an open mind

Armed with a lot of questions

I head out to his office

To meet him, to greet him

To learn from him!

With admiration & affection

Doubt and temptation,

I introduce myself

I am Mukesh & I want to know

About starting and running a business

What to do & what to avoid

When to start & when to stop

I have a lot of questions

For which I seek answers

So that I and my friends

Can start and run businesses

With more success than failure

Spreading more joy than sadness!

The Why!

He looks at me

His eyes so kind

With a voice so soft

He asks:

    "But why do you want to start a business?"

I say:

"How does it matter?

Is it important to know the answer?

What difference does it make

If I want to make more money or name

or if I want to create more jobs

or if I want to "Make a dent in the universe"

what difference does it make?

He says:

    It makes as much difference

    As it makes to plant the right seed

    If you want apples, you need to plant an apple seed

    You need to plough your field for an apple tree

    Sow the seeds of an apple tree

    Apply the right manure and prepare the field

> So that you can grow an apple tree
>
> If you want to harvest within the year
>
> Apple tree is not for you my dear

This I understand sir.

I want to start a business

To make money and help countless others

Who need jobs ;

To matter and to leave a legacy,

That's the reason, I want to learn

More about starting a business.

The When

Now that this is clear

Can you tell me sir

When is the right time to start a business

Is it when I am young, fresh out-of-college

With a fresh mind and no responsibilities

Or is it better to work for someone else

To Learn on the job

To make your share of mistakes

On someone else's cost

Though it may mean you spend some years

And end with more Responsibilities in life

Or is it when my hair is grey and

My heir is turning young

When is the right time to start a business sir?

He says:

    Just like there is no age to learn

    No age to die

    There is no age to start a business

    Some start young

    Some not so young

    If you do all it takes,

    It's never too soon

    Nor too late!

Hmm, now I understand sir

As with everything else in life

It doesn't matter when you start, where you start

What matters is what you start, how you start

And whether you finish, whatever you start!

The How

Now that I know, it doesn't matter when you start

Please tell me what do I need to start

Do I need money or ideas?

Do I need a team or should I go alone?

What should I know and what should I do?

He says:

> To start a business my dear
>
> You don't need money nor idea
>
> You don't need team or any thing else
>
> To start a business my dear
>
> All you need is a "Will-to-win" & an "open mind"
>
> With a will-to-win and an open mind
>
> Everything else is a matter of time
>
> Cometh the hour, cometh the money
>
> Cometh the hour, cometh the idea
>
> Cometh the hour, cometh the team

This is so good sir,

Once I have an open mind

And a will-to-win

What do I do next?

He says:

> Let's get back to my question
>
> Sit back and think about the reason
>
> Why do you want to start a business?
>
> Now, write that down on a piece of paper
>
> Fold it & keep it in your wallet
>
> Now, don't you ever forget that piece of paper
>
> Take it out, read it aloud
>
> At every step of the way
>
> When the options are clear
>
> And the choice not so clear
>
> This piece of paper is your guiding light
>
> This will take your ship to your port all right!
>
> Now that you have your guiding light
>
> With an open mind, start thinking all night
>
> Come up with ideas about business you want to start
>
> And then write them all
>
> Keep up the thinking with an open mind
>
> And Don't bother with all the crap that you write
>
> Take a few days, take a few weeks
>
> Till you hit an idea and that hits you

    One that is impossible to do

    One that doesn't leave you

    That my dear is the business

    You need to do!

Hmm, Now I understand

The business idea comes from the knowledge of what I want

And is not based on logic or thought

But based on the feeling of my gut!

I am not sure if that is the way

As I am not sure if my gut will show me the way

How do I get over this doubt

Help me sir, with your thought!

He says:

    The thing you call your gut,

    Is not just your gut

    It's your connection to your inner-self

    It's your connection to yourself

    The more you trust your gut

    The more you trust yourself

    The more you trust yourself

    The more calm and happy you get

> That's that state that our God wants for us.
>
> So my dear, throw your doubts aside
>
> And think with an open mind
>
> The one thought that sticks to your mind
>
> Could be the one that unlocks your soul
>
> Treat it with respect & so it shall treat you
>
> Once decided, have a will to win
>
> And get started on the way to win!

Hmm, now I understand

With an open mind,

A will to win and a

Business close to your heart

Theres only one thing

That could stop you

And that is YOU!

He says:

> That's right! Nicely said!
>
> With a fire in the belly
>
> An open mind, a will to win
>
> And a cause that's close to heart
>
> All the Gods are with you

And the only thing that can stop you

Is Only YOU!

Product or Service

I ask - Is it better to have build a product or a service?

He says:

> It is not a either product or service
>
> Best way is for you to start with a service
>
> So you can build a product
>
> Services are the oxygen that allow you
>
> To grow and build products.
>
> Products when done right
>
> Can let your business take flight!

Hmm.. So, till we take flight with a product

Offering Services gives us a safety net!

Building a Product

Help me understand how to build a product

That can let my business take flight

He says:

> Build a product
>
> for yourself
>
> or for someone you know.
>
> For trying to build for everyone
>
> Will result in building for none

All Great products have something in common

- Has the Customer's best interest at heart
- Fulfills an existing desire
- Evoke a specific emotion
- And in the process create a habit

Before your build, test and iterate

Understand the desire you want to fulfill

Understand the emotion you want to evoke

And figure out the habit you want to create

Hmm, I understand the importance of

Customer's best interest at heart,

To a certain extent also the need to fulfill a desire part

But can you please explain the significance of the emotion and the habit part?

He says:

> We humans are a creature of emotions
>
> At the root of every successful product,
>
> There is a strong emotion that exists
>
> Dig deep enough and you will find it.
>
> Even among emotions,
>
> Avoiding negative emotions is better
>
> Than reinforcing positive emotions

When we talk about habits,

There are three parts to it

- See
- Do
- Feel

Show what you want them to do

Help them do it

Reward them for doing it

Integrate these in your product

Increase your odds of success !

Hmm...

So, To have a successful product

I need to be able to fulfill a desire

Which leads to an emotion

And do it well enough to make this a habit!

FUNDING

Now that I have an product idea

That's close to my heart and soul

Which evokes the right feeling

And creates a habit

That is right for my customer,

How do I get the money

And let the ball roll

He says:

> There are 3 sources of money
>
> > Your Money
> >
> > Their money
> >
> > Someone else's money
>
> Your money is the money you have
>
> Their money is their own money
>
> Someone else's money is somebody's money,
>
> No one knows whose money.
>
> Each kind has its own vices and nices
>
> *To start a business*, its best to use your own money
>
> But make sure you don't use all your money
>
> Being a miser, is wiser

Better to be a miser at the start than to

Close your business without a shot

Anticipate your expenses

Double it and prepare yourself

Find ways to cut your cost

And spend as less as you can

With a creative mind, you can find ways

To pay in kind instead of cash

To barter something instead of paying by cash

To provide a service instead of cash

The more you do this at the beginning

The better chances you have at finishing

Barter, Bargain & pay in kind

To keep your costs down

Never offer equity at this stage on.

The time to go looking for "_Their Money_"

Is when you need money to stay afloat

And to manage your cash flow

It's better to borrow this money than sell equity

As it is their money, managed by themselves

He will want the most out of it and so

Will cut you a deal that will suit him more

Better to borrow from him than to sell!

The time to get "*Somebody's money*" is

When you have options to grow

Opportunities galore

And its cash that stops you

And it's time to grow

Then my dear it's time to get "*somebody's money*"

Somebody's money is managed by some-one else

To keep getting somebody's money

He needs to show a good return

So he seeks out those who seek to grow

And fast growth is where his heart goes!

This is the time when you decide

If you want to keep going

If you want to take a dig and move out

Go looking for pastures

That could be closer to your heart

Than the one that started it all!

When taking somebody's money

Never take the deal offered to you

It's always better to haggle a bit

And sure, you will get a better deal

See, they are dealing not with their own money

But somebody's money

So negotiate they will

And offer a better deal

When you haggle with them over the deal!

Hmm, now I understand

The difference between my own money

Their money and somebody else's money

And also when to use which money

Building a team

Tell me o Sir, when is the time to go looking out

And get a team which would work out

He says:

> That's a great topic that you have brought up
>
> One that's most difficult for a start-up
>
> The best time to build a team
>
> Is when you are getting started-up
>
> Delay it a bit and you might not have a start-up
>
> Get it wrong and for sure you will not have a start-up
>
> This is one of those things
>
> that could either destroy
>
> Or give a new-lease of life

Hmm, I understand this now

The time to put together a team

The earlier the better, it is now!

Hiring

Could you also tell me sir

The qualities I should look

When building the team

He says:

Look for people who are

    "Passionate about something

    Who have a lot of friends?

    Who have tried different things"

Everything else is a plus

Could you please unpack that ?

What's special about these three traits?

He says:

    When somebody is passionate about something

    They know what passion is and what it could do

    It's easier to ignite passion in passionate people

    Someone with a lot of friends

    Knows to move with people

    Knows when to chip in

    When to move out of the way

    He can work with anyone

    He can gel with everyone

    He will be a team player

    One of the kind, you would want

    If he has tried different things

    Knows what it's like to venture in the unknown

> More willing to learn & un-learn
>
> Would have seen people fail
>
> And knows it is ok to fail
>
> With these traits
>
> Its very hard to say
>
> No to success!

Hmm, I understand this now

Passionate, friendly and one with an open mind

Is the recipe to look for in an ideal employee

Treating your team

Now that we talk about team & employee,

Could you also tell me the way to treat them fairly?

Is an annual appraisal program, the right way to groom them all?

He says:

> Annual appraisal is what everyone does
>
> I am afraid it doesn't work well
>
> I think it is best to appraise people
>
> As and when they perform
>
> Praise them, reprise them
>
> As soon as they

Did something right or wrong

If you think they are ready to move up the ladder

To take up more responsibility

To lead and succeed,

Do not wait for the year to end

But give them the responsibility

Right there and then

You will find people are happier

And the morale high!

When they see others succeed

While doing something right

Note that I have said more responsibility

And not a promotion

For promotions are why

Teams break up

For promotions are limited

So, seeds of jealousy they sow

And team work – there it goes.

If you want to use promotions,

I suggest you rather promote a team

Than any individual

> As then the team becomes important
>
> Than any single individual!

Hmm, now I understand

If you promote an individual

You get a team full of individuals

When you promote a team

You get teams made up of members!

Firing

What do we do if there is a wrong hire

And we have to fire the hire?

He says:

> There are three reasons to fire a hire
>
> Atleast two must be true before you fire
>
> Wrong Attitude, mismatch of expectations
>
> And unwilling to act on feedback
>
> If she exhibits the wrong attitude,
>
> Talk to the hire and give feedback
>
> Fire if things don't change quickly.
>
> Be slow to hire and quick to fire

Key to stay in business

Now could you tell me sir,

What all I need to remember

When I run my business

What is the key

To keep it running?

He says:

>First rule:
>
>>Manage your cash flow
>>
>>Failing which you will not
>>
>>Have a business to grow!
>
>Second rule:
>
>>Manager your customers experience
>>
>>Without whom you will not have a business to experience
>
>Third Rule:
>
>>Keep your employees happy
>>
>>In order to keep your customers happy

Could you please elaborate?

So that it is easy for me to assimilate!

First Rule – Manage Cash Flow

He says:

> Cash flow is like your heart & blood
>
> As long as it is sufficient
>
> No-one notices its presence
>
> The moment it dries up,
>
> There is no one left to notice its absence
>
> So, if you want to sell a product or a service
>
> Create it, put it in the market
>
> Start selling it so that the cash flows in
>
> Earlier the better
>
> If the product is not ready
>
> Use an open mind and think of
>
> Ways to keep the cash coming
>
> Beg, borrow, barter, bargain
>
> Do anything to keep the cash coming
>
> Cut your costs, find ways
>
> to limit cash going out!
>
> Pump more of 'your money' in
>
> Get their money if required
>
> But keep the cash flowing
>
> For, Till the heart beats

And the blood circulates

We live to fight yet another day

Second Rule – Manage Customer Experience

Manage your customer's experience

Note that I've not said – sell or service your customer

But to manage your customer's experience

In order to succeed and thrive in a business

You need to manage your customer's experience

Their exploring experience,

Buying experience

Using experience

After sale service experience

Their in-store experience

Their competition experience

To succeed in today's world

Selling and servicing your customer well

Is Necessary But not sufficient!

You need to be obsessed with their

Experiences

That, my dear is the only way

To succeed in a business!

Third Rule – Manage Employee Happiness:

> Keep your employees happy
>
> Not only because they create the experiences for your customers
>
> Not only because they are your eyes & ears in the marketplace
>
> Not only because happy employees are more productive than the rest
>
> Not only because it is the best thing to do for your business
>
> But more importantly because
>
> They are also people,
>
> Just like you and me
>
> And they deserve to be happy
>
> Just like you and me!

Hmm, now I understand

The importance of the 3 rules sir

One is to keep you running

Two is to get you winning

Three is to get you smiling!

Compensation

Now that we are talking about

Keeping employees happy

Could you tell me how to pay them?

So they remain happy?

He says:

> But money is just one part of the salary you should pay
>
> Pay her respect for the job she does
>
> Pay her with your time & feedback so she may improve her skills
>
> Pay her with a great team to work with so she may make friends for life
>
> Pay her with a great challenge, so she could push her limits to re-discover herself
>
> Pay her with seed money and
>
> A word of encouragement
>
> If she wants to start her own business!
>
> But pay her enough money so she can
>
> Forget about the money
>
> And start thinking about
>
> Everything else that you pay her as well!

Hmm, now I understand sir

Pay her enough money

To take care of her physical needs

Pay her in kind

To take care of her emotional needs

Pay her in spirit

To take care of her spiritual needs!

Competition

Could you also tell me sir

How do I handle competition?

He says:

> Competition is like your brother dear
>
> He helps you increase the pie!
>
> Never go after a competitor
>
> Go after a product or a market
>
> Or better still go after a customer
>
> Don't you focus on activities
>
> To handle competition
>
> Instead, focus on your customer's experience!
>
> Competition is not the enemy
>
> Nor is it bad!
>
> Complacency is the enemy
>
> And it definitely is bad!
>
> See your competition as your energy drink
>
> The more the merrier
>
> Among the competition
>
> Seek out a path exclusively for yourself
>
> Be open to share your knowledge

Be open to learn from them,

To work with them!

Keep your eyes & ears open

And with an open mind

Look for opportunities that they

Give a-miss

As it could open up markets

And profits

Seek out ways to convert

Your competition as your customers

As it is a better strategy

To consult & co-exist

Rather than compete & perish!

Hmm, now I understand sir

Treat your competitors as friends

Who happen to run a similar business

Seek out ways to co-operate and co-exist

Rather than compete & perish!

Winding up

Could you also help me sir

On when to know my time is up?

He says:

> You know that it's time for you to cash-out
>
> When you do not feel the same
>
> About the business when you started out
>
> And the business has grown enough
>
> And someone is bothered by your business
>
> To buy you out
>
> You know that it's time to move out
>
> When you don't feel the same way
>
> About the business as you felt
>
> When you started out
>
> And the business is not grown enough
>
> To be sold out
>
> You find someone who is passionate
>
> About the business
>
> One who can take the business
>
> To its logical conclusion
>
> Then hand-it-over to him

And then you move-out!

As you are still invested

Continue to spend sometime

And monitor the progress

But your time is better invested

In something else.

You know that it's time to close out

When despite all your efforts

The cash isn't flowing-in

Maybe customers aren't ready yet

Or the market for that

When despite the best team

Putting their best efforts

Things don't improve for

6 straight quarters

You know it's time

for you to close-out & move on!

Hmm, now I understand sir,

If you have a successful business

But don't feel passionate about it

It's time to cash-out!

If you have a potentially successful business

But don't feel passionate about it

It's time to move-out!

If you have an un-successful business

And don't feel passionate about it

It's time to close out!

Could you also help me sir

To learn how to treat my team

If I decide to cash-out, move out or close out!

He says:

    When you plan to cash out

    Inform your team before they

    Get to know it from anyone else

    Try to provide them an option

    To cash out with you as well!

    When you plan to move out

    Let them all know that

    Your heart beats for someplace else

    That you have identified a leader

    Who in all Ernest is able, capable

    Who shall lead them to greater success

That you shall still be involved

And will be available should someone need

Wish them success & joy in their journey!

Most important of all - stay true to your words!

When you plan to close-out

Let them all know early in time

Talk to them about with honesty

About the situation & the necessity

Share what you plan to do

And how it affects them

Share what you plan to do

Once you close out

See if they could join you in

Your next journey!

Most important thing you could do

Is to give them enough time!

Most important of all

Whatever the situation

Treat them all with

The respect they deserve

For they were with you

    Shoulder-to-shoulder

    Walking with you,

    Day-after-day, year-after-year

    In A journey that you started

    They deserve all the

    Respect and dignity you could give!

Hmm, now I understand sir,

No matter what the situation

Treat them fair,

With respect & dignity

As they were with you

On your journey so far!

Thanks

Thank you sir

For sharing your wisdom

Out I will go & start my business

Following the path

That you have shown!

Will return to you when

I need some help or

When my journey ends!

Thank you sir

For all your wisdom!!!!

www.ingramcontent.com/pod-product-compliance
Lightning Source LLC
Chambersburg PA
CBHW020713180526
45163CB00008B/3067